The First of Everso

STORY BY ELIZABETH BOLEMAN-HERRING

ILLUSTRATIONS AND PAPER DOLLS BY SANDRA TICE-WRIGHT

BOOK DESIGN BY GARETH WALTERS

Published by
The Literate Chigger Press, Inc.
1175 Queen Anne Road,
Teaneck, New Jersey 07666
Tel/Fax: (201) 862-0975
literatechigger@earthlink.net
www.tlcpress.com
www.greecetraveler.com

Printed in Hong Kong.

Number _33_ of 1,000 limited first edition copies

Library of Congress
Cataloging-in-Publication Data
Boleman-Herring, Elizabeth   The First of Everso
Story by Elizabeth Boleman-Herring;
Illustrations and paper dolls by Sandra Tice-Wright.

**Summary: In Dreams-upon-Waking, where each subject has
one single wish come true, selfish, shortsighted wishes for
beauty, wealth and power are shown to be inferior to wishes
for wisdom, enlightenment and the greater good of others.**

1. Children's fairy tale–fiction.
2. Selfish desires vs. altruism–fiction.
I. Tice-Wright, Sandra, ill. II. Title.

First Edition

This story is for those who have chosen to be beautiful,
and for those who have chosen not to be.

The Literate Chigger Press
Teaneck, New Jersey

edicated to the author's beloved parents,
Beth and Jack; the artist's beautiful models,
Ben and Hannah; and the designer's lovely and
courageous mother, Patricia Elizabeth Walters.

 f you open your grand-mother's encyclopedia or atlas or even her very good red, fabric-covered dictionary, you may find a map of the world.

But on no map of the world, not even in these old, worn books, will you ever find the tiny kingdom of Dreams-upon-Waking because, years and years and years ago, even before your great grandparents' time, Dreams-upon-Waking was conquered by a neighboring kingdom and renamed something dull, like Green-land, or Eng-land or Hol-land.

But, while it existed, Dreams-upon-Waking, much better known to us as Dreamland, was a very peculiar place indeed, and the people who lived there, their children's children's grandchildren now scattered to the four corners of the earth, were very peculiar people. Even the animals and household objects and the frog-green River Waking, which flowed through Dreams-upon-Waking, were peculiar, but we

will come to all that in good time.

About all that survives of the peculiar and beautiful Kingdom of Dreamland is the story I am about to tell you, which was told to me over the course of several evenings when I was a little girl, just before I went to bed.

In those days I was in the habit of asking my mother to bring me a little glass of ginger ale, and then a little glass of milk, and finally a little glass of water, in succession, and then to tell me a very long story, or I would not go to sleep at night. I was an only child whom all my aunts and uncles said was very spoiled. But, in truth, I was only a very lonely child, and wanted to keep my mother in my room as long as I could every night because I was afraid of sleeping by myself in the dark.

If I had been a more perceptive child, I would have noticed that most bad things happen to us during the daytime and not when we are asleep in bed right next to our mothers' and fathers' rooms, but by the time I had figured that out I was already grown up and wasn't afraid of the dark any more.

ut to get back to my mother's bedtime story, it was about this peculiar kingdom I have told you about already, a kingdom where dreams came true.

They did not always come true easily, I should add. My mother told me that in order to make a dream come true a person, or an object, even, in Dreams-upon-Waking might have to work very hard indeed, and be very patient. But eventually, except in a few cases, your dream would come true. You would have your heart's desire.

But there was, said Mother, a catch. (There is always a catch.) Every creature and every thing (and even the River Waking) in this tiny landlocked kingdom was allowed only one dream. So you had to be very, very careful in choosing your dream, because it was the only one you could be sure would come true. (You may have heard another story about a genie who granted someone three wishes: That genie did not live in Dreams-upon-Waking, I can assure you. No one granted anyone else any wishes, and everyone dreamed her, or his, own dream in Dreamland.)

Oh, and there was something else, said my mother. You were not required to tell anyone your dream if you didn't want to. You could keep it a secret. You could write it on a scrap of paper and wear it in a locket around your neck. You could write it, in China ink,

on a round, white pebble, and bury it in the ground. You could whisper it to the River Waking when you waded there in hottest Everso, the month between July and August. Or, you could hide it deep in your heart and tell no one, not even your own mother. That special dream of yours was yours alone. Eventually, of course, when your dream came true, most people would realize what it was. In the pudding was the proof, so to speak. But until the day that your black curls turned strawberry blonde or you could compose operas as well as little Wolfgang Amadeus Mozart or write fairy tales as well as my mother could tell them, say, then you could keep your dream to yourself.

Oh yes, there were two other catches. Unfortunately, or fortunately, who can tell, in Dreams-upon-Waking, a human being's dream was always more powerful than that of an object. Toys and mirrors and bars of chocolate might dream dreams, it is true, but their owners' wishes could override them. If they resisted, they could be smashed or thrown away and replaced, or even eaten. And that, as they say, was that.

Also, if two subjects of Dreamland cherished conflicting dreams, the law decreed that they walk off in precisely opposite directions for a day's journey and stay there to avoid any unpleasantness. This had happened only once, however, when two

little boys dreamed of becoming the King of Dreamland. There was only one king in Dreams-upon-Waking, and it was he who finally sent one little boy off to the west and one to the east. The boys did eventually become kings, but of two rather small, boring kingdoms where they had no subjects to rule and no queens with whom to play Scrabble or checkers. They had not chosen their dreams well at all, you see.

he King of Dreams-upon-Waking, who was very fat, very short, as ugly as a beet root and just about as red, had dreamed, for a very long time, of having a beautiful daughter, the most beautiful little girl ever to live in Dreamland. The Queen, who was herself short, fat, red, and as homely as a radish, also dreamed of having a beautiful daughter. So the royal couple had not given up hope even after having ten ugly daughters and ten uglier sons. This was Dreams-upon-Waking, they reasoned, and their dreams would eventually come true.

My mother said that as early as twenty years before the Princess's birth, the King and Queen had decided to name her Elspeth. And when the child was finally born, as lovely as a white and pink and chocolate-covered rose – she had chestnut curls – there were great celebrations in the castle on the River Waking. (The river itself had a very simple dream. It dreamed it would forever get everyone's toes wet in the month of Everso, a dream that came true, like clockwork, once a year.)

Elspeth was a beautiful, beautiful baby, indeed, and a beautiful, beautiful little girl, and by the time she was thirteen, she took everyone's breath away she was so beautiful. But the poor King and Queen, and her twenty ugly brothers and sisters were all most unhappy in the castle, because beautiful Elspeth had a personality rather like that of Tyrannosaurus Rex, a now extinct giant reptile that walked the earth during the Cretaceous period, if you must know. Elspeth

was horrid. Elspeth was selfish. Elspeth was cruel. You may know someone just like her.

And her dream, which she decided upon very early in life, was to make everyone and everything in Dreamland do exactly as she wanted. She was a clever little girl and it was a clever little dream, but it was destined to make a great many people and things quite miserable, and it was to be the ruination of many of the kingdom's official toy maker's most lovely creations.

he toy maker, whose great talent lay in making life sized porcelain dolls, was a proud, tall man whose wife had died some years before, leaving him with a daughter who was, to tell the truth, as plain as a plain white plate. But Dogwood – that was her name – was as graceful as her mother had been, and as quiet as a tree, and her father loved her more than his life. She was that rare thing, a kind and tender little girl, and her father wished he could fashion her a beautiful, porcelain face to go with her great good heart.

But, unfortunately, this wish could not be granted, as the toy maker had chosen his dream years before Dogwood's birth. The toy maker's dream was to make toys and dolls that rich buyers, and especially those in the royal household, where twenty-one children

had played with his creations, could not resist. The coins of the kingdom were called Dreamlanders, and Tom the toy maker had more Dreamlanders in the bank than anyone in Dreamland except, of course, the King. His shop was, as a result, almost always empty, and little Dogwood, who was not a rich buyer, had never had a toy or a doll of her very own.

In fact, most always, because she was so plain and so quiet, her father kept her out of sight, hidden away in a basement room among all his bolts of satin and round, China-blue dolls' eyes and needles and stuffing and thread. Here, Dogwood was a great help to her father, stitching up the dolls' clothes and fitting the leather hooves on the rocking horses. And here, too, she would not be seen by the King of Dreamland whenever he happened by with his beautiful daughter Elspeth.

For some reason, it disquieted the King to see Dogwood, who was so plain and quiet and dear, and the toy maker had made a point of shooing her out of the shop and downstairs whenever the sounds of the King's horses and carriage were heard in the street.

From her basement window, though, Dogwood always awaited the King's arrival with great joy, for it almost always meant she would see Elspeth. Looking up, with her wide-set, earnest brown eyes, she would start at the Princess's perfect patent leather shoes,

4

and then, slowly and shyly, take in a picture of beauty she always found almost too good to be real.

Elspeth was thirteen the year she was given her last toy from the toy maker's shop, and in her twelfth year she had become more lovely, more radiant than ever before. Her patent leather shoes now had tiny heels, and her stockings were made of the finest Belgian lace. She wore a matching white lace dress covered with seed pearls, and a green silk ribbon around her waist. There were pearls at her white throat, and her chestnut curls fell down her back like shining chocolate syrup, and bounced as she walked. She hadn't got used to her heels yet but, leaning on her father's arm for support, she was even more beautiful for being a little clumsy. To look into Elspeth's celery-green eyes was an experience no one forgot, ever. Dogwood used to look at her face in wonder, close her eyes tight, and pretend she was looking into a mirror. Since the toy maker kept no mirrors in the shop, nor in the lovely cottage he was building for

Dogwood next door, the girl had been spared the sight of her own uninteresting face.

On the occasion of the King's final visit to the toy maker, he was in quite a state. Elspeth, leaning on his arm, had complained all the way down from the castle that she really didn't want any more toys. Oh yes, she said, when she first saw them she wanted them very much. But when she got them home to her room at the very top of the castle's highest tower, there always seemed to be something wrong with them.

"It's true, Father," she drawled in her irritating, bored voice. "They just will not do as I say. That ballerina doll, for instance. I commanded it to sing the aria from *The Marriage of Figaro*, and yet all it could do was pirouette round and round on one stupid toe. Do you blame me for tossing it out the window, silly pink tutu, toe shoes and all?"

"But my dear," said the miserable King, "That ballerina, an exact replica of the beautiful Pavlova, cost me all of seven hundred and twenty Dreamlanders. She

couldn't help it if her dream was to dance and dance and dance. Oh why can't you ever let anything be?" he sighed, and Elspeth smiled to herself, for she knew her own dream was more powerful than that of any handmade, mechanical toy.

"Then there was that idiotic rocking horse that wouldn't do anything but rock, back and forth, back and forth, back and forth. It just about drove me crazy watching that fool animal. I wanted it to jump through a hoop for me. Just a simple little jump. Was that too much to ask?"

"Well, it did finally jump, didn't it?" scowled the King. "Right out your turret window and down with a thud on the lawn. It broke neatly in half, got its stuffing soaked in the rain, and then it just disappeared! Eight hundred Dreamlanders for that horse and it just vanished into thin air."

"Probably rocked its way across the border," smirked Elspeth. She really could be most disagreeable.

"And the toy soldier? Whatever was wrong with him?" asked the King. "He was noble and upright and had a gallant grey moustache and . . ."

". . . he was as boring as a turnip," snapped the Princess. "I asked him to salute me whenever I entered the room, but all he could do was stand to attention and say he was protecting the crown. 'I am sworn to protect the crown, Your Grace!' – his very words! Honestly, what did you expect me to do? It was like having a parrot in my room – that one ridiculous sentence over and over and over . . ."

"So you pushed him out the window, too! Oh, he was a pitiful sight! One thousand Dreamlanders! Gold buttons, gold braid, gold sword bent in two! Elspeth, you really are going to ruin me. But you're so beautiful that I can't bring myself to scold you any more. Let's go in and see what my fine friend the toy maker has for us today. It may be something too big to go through your window."

ogwood, from her own window in the basement, had watched this scene with great concentration, her serene brow as round as an eggshell, her hair pulled back from her face and tied with a piece of blue yarn.

The instant that Elspeth had mentioned the ballerina, though, Dogwood had silently drawn the curtains and had continued watching the King and the little Princess through a hole in the lace. For in a dark corner of the basement workshop where she stitched the dolls' clothes, the ballerina stood practicing her pirouettes. And in the corner opposite rocked the rocking horse. Behind it the toy soldier stood to attention, his gold

buttons shining, his moustache as perfect as the day the toy maker had sent him home to guard Elspeth's turret door.

For Dogwood knew of Elspeth's temper as, indeed, did every subject throughout the entire kingdom of Dreams-upon-Waking. And when a toy came plummeting down from that high, bright window, Dogwood would be waiting to carry the pieces back to the toyshop's basement.

Over time, she had repaired each and every one of the Princess's discarded toys, but she never played with them. She had retrieved and restored them, and cherished them in the hope that, some day, Elspeth

would change her mind and want them back.

If Elspeth was too beautiful to be quite real, Dogwood was too good. But if it doesn't seem fair that Elspeth got all the toys and Dogwood did all the work and had no toys, it's only because these two little girls were to dream quite different dreams.

Dogwood hadn't chosen her dream as yet, but she pondered it constantly. It had something to do, she knew, with loving and cherishing and nurturing, but she felt she hadn't got it quite right yet, so she'd put off her decision. In the meantime, she had rejected a great many dreams she felt might be too small, too meager. As she grew older, it seemed to become more and more difficult to make a choice.

When her father gently teased her, asking her to tell him her dream, just to whisper it in his ear, she said only, "Don't worry, Daddy. It's a dream that will grow up with me." That was all she would ever say, but it was enough for her father.

"Poor, homely, good little Dogwood," he would always think to himself. "I'm sure you have a homely, good little dream. But don't worry. With all the thousands and thousands of Dreamlanders the King and Queen have spent on our toys, you'll always have a roof over your head, shoes on your feet, and more than enough to eat."

nd so it was visions of more and more Dreamlanders, those pancake-sized coins of beaten gold stamped with the King's grandfather's father's grandfather's portly form, that swam before his eyes as he went out and bowed low before his beet-colored monarch.

"Your Grace, Princess Elspeth, how may I be of service today?" sang the toy maker.

"Well, since your shop's totally empty," shot back Elspeth, glancing around the deserted store, "I don't see that you can be of any service at all."

"Now, Elspeth," said the King, miserably, and, "I'm sorry, Tom. She's just impatient with me today. My daughter thinks she's too grown up for toys now and, I must say, after all the exquisite things she's thrown out her tenth story window, I wouldn't blame you if you never made another doll for my ungrateful, beautiful brat. I should have built her rooms on the first floor. But, you see, her thirteenth birthday's coming up . . ."

The toy maker smiled gently and went over to a narrow drawer where he kept the rolled up parchments on which he drew his designs. He had been waiting for just this moment as he had an idea for a doll he felt sure Elspeth, not to speak of her father, would find irresistible. For the King to see his daughter's face light up with wonder and desire was a rare and matchless experience. It gave him some hope that her beautiful countenance would not always be discontented, bored or angry. For the King, a smile on Elspeth's lips was like summer sunshine on a cat's back, and Tom felt sure he had just the thing in mind to produce a whole summer of smiles.

The King reached out his pudgy hands and took a parchment from the toy maker. As it fell open, he saw an elegant drawing. It was a beautiful princeling, a youth so perfect, so graceful, and so very like Elspeth herself, that both the King and his youngest child were speechless.

Tom broke the silence. "So, you like him?" Of course, given the toy maker's dream, it was inevitable that this should be true, but this time, dream or no dream, the Princess was humbled, enchanted.

"Oh, Daddy," whispered the beautiful Elspeth. "I must have him. I must! Where is he, Tom? Where have you hidden him?"

But the toy maker barred the door to the basement before Elspeth could dash down the steps into the workshop. "He's not ready, Princess. It will take months to prepare his body, his clothes, his face. I've sent off leagues and leagues to the west and the east, the south and the north, for the finest cloth of gold, the softest kid leather, the purest, most translucent porcelain. And, just before your birthday, in Everso, I shall assemble his

precious ruby heart at the very last moment. But I promise that he will be ready for your birthday. I give you my word. If Dogwood and I have to work our fingers to the bone, you shall have your prince before the great day."

Elspeth went out into the street beaming with anticipation, and all those who saw her over the next few months were amazed at the transformation in her character. She was happy and full of hope, and the joy of the castle and kingdom, where preparations were underway for her annual birthday party.

"Oh, he will be everything my heart desires," sighed Elspeth in her empty turret room. "He could be my twin in porcelain," she said, pink cheek in hand, "and whatever I tell him to do I know he will do, just to make me happy."

eanwhile, back in the toy maker's basement workshop, Dogwood and her father were hard at work. Tom, the master craftsman, first fashioned the prince's perfect body out of the finest porcelain, jointing the limbs so cunningly that, for all the world, the young prince seemed real.

The prince was as tall as Dogwood, who was a bit on the tall side and skinny as a rail, and much taller than Elspeth. "The Princess will have a hard time tossing this fellow out her window," chuckled Tom.

Dogwood, who loved helping her father, sat by his side at the work table and stitched the prince's stockings, his trousers, his waistcoat, his lace stock, his coat and his gloves. She even stitched his fine leather shoes and his powdered wig, and it was Dogwood who, with her camel's hair brushes, put the finest blush on the prince's cheeks and the red on his lips.

As they worked, the toy maker talked to the prince, whom he had named Aethelred, but whom his daughter called Redwood, telling him all about Elspeth, the castle, the King and Queen, and the life he would lead in the tall turret and great halls of the fortress. Needless to say, Tom left out all the bits about toys falling out of tall windows, and if Dogwood harbored any fears about Prince Redwood's fate, she buried them deep in her heart.

The rocking horse, the toy soldier and the ballerina, hidden out of sight behind a Javanese screen in the far corner, kept silent while Tom was in the room, and Dogwood made them promise not to tell the princeling about the less than perfect side of Elspeth's character.

"I'm sure he will choose his dream more carefully than you," she said to them, "though your dreams were fine ones. And if she is happy with him, and he with her, then I am certain it will all work out for the

best." The rocking horse, who had a sense of foreboding, mumbled something about packing a parachute in the prince's luggage, just in case, but Dogwood was too distracted by her endless sewing to take any notice.

Still, as she tinted the prince's cheeks, rubbed his shoes to make them shine, and looked into his celery-colored eyes with their magnificent black lashes – so very like the little Princess's eyes – she felt a sense of loss and fear. But she said nothing.

The prince, who was not as quiet as Dogwood, began conversing with the toy maker and his daughter as soon as his mouth was finished. In Dreamland, all toys could speak, and they made as much sense as most of the people.

Tom, who described Elspeth over and over for Aethelred, had almost succeeded in making the doll feel something like love for her. The prince looked forward to living in her beautiful turret rooms which overlooked the entire kingdom and the whole length of the wide, green River Waking. Prince Aethelred felt no toy would ever be as fortunate as he, no real prince as handsome, no human being as true. He was not puffed up or proud exactly, but just hopeful in the way all those in love for the first time are hopeful.

Since Dogwood, patient and kind and dear and selfless, had counseled him to choose his dream carefully – as though his very existence depended upon its being a good dream, she had said – he was pondering the choice with great seriousness. Finally, one night, when the toy maker's daughter had fallen asleep over his half-finished satin tunic, he bent down and whispered in her ear.

"Dogwood! Sweet, plain, skinny Dogwood! I know you can't hear me, but I've decided upon my dream. My only wish will be to love and serve the most perfect creature in all of Dreams-upon-Waking, to live beside only her who is worthy of a perfect princeling's love and devotion! Whatever perfection I possess I owe to you and your father; in accepting the responsibility for this dream, perhaps I can repay you both for your great gifts to me."

Prince Aethelred felt this dream was an inspiration. It was noble and good, he thought, and he was certain it would please Elspeth, whom he knew would be as perfect as Tom the toy maker had promised. After all, hadn't he, the faithful, true and flawless Prince Aethelred, been made in the Princess's image?

The rocking horse, rocking silently in its corner, unable to sleep, heard Aethelred's words and shuddered, remembering all too clearly that sickening, sudden descent from the Princess's window. "Oh dear," it sighed, as it rocked itself to sleep. "Oh dear! Oh dear!"

The morning after Prince Aethelred

had whispered his dream to the sleeping Dogwood, the sun came up in the west, as it did in those days, and everyone trooped down to cool their feet in the River Waking, which gurgled with delight among the thousands of wriggling toes.

It was the first day of the month of Everso, the brightest, clearest, warmest day of the year, by royal decree. It was the Princess Elspeth's thirteenth birthday. All the subjects of Dreams-upon-Waking had been busy for weeks, cleaning and whitewashing their homes and baking pies and cakes and cookies and special crown-shaped cinnamon buns to take to the Princess's birthday picnic.

Each year on this day the King and Queen invited everyone in the kingdom to a vast party on the banks of the River Waking. There were dancers and singers and lots of fruit punch, and there were fireworks from dusk to dawn. Early in the evening, the monarch always presented his youngest daughter with a special birthday present, and there were, as well, rich gifts for all the kingdom's children

under fourteen, so no little ones ever felt left out. "Elspeth's birthday belongs to all of us," announced the King every year, "because it was a dream come true."

Dogwood, who had slept only a few hours at the workshop table, her head on her arm, woke up late and then hurried to prepare Prince Aethelred for his journey to the castle. Aethelred, rested but excited, and dressed in a violet dressing gown, looked into Dogwood's earnest, tired eyes and then seized her by her bony little shoulders. Dogwood blinked in surprise but, for the thousandth time, reminded herself that Redwood was only a doll, beautiful, but just another of her father's creations. Still, he seemed so real.

"Oh Dogwood, wake up, you sleepyhead! Smile!" he cried. "Are you not happy for me? Today I will meet the Princess Elspeth and my dream will begin to come true. Please, Dogwood, smile for me. I am so, so grateful to you for all your work; for making possible this great happiness that I feel."

"Come, come, Aethelred," said Tom,

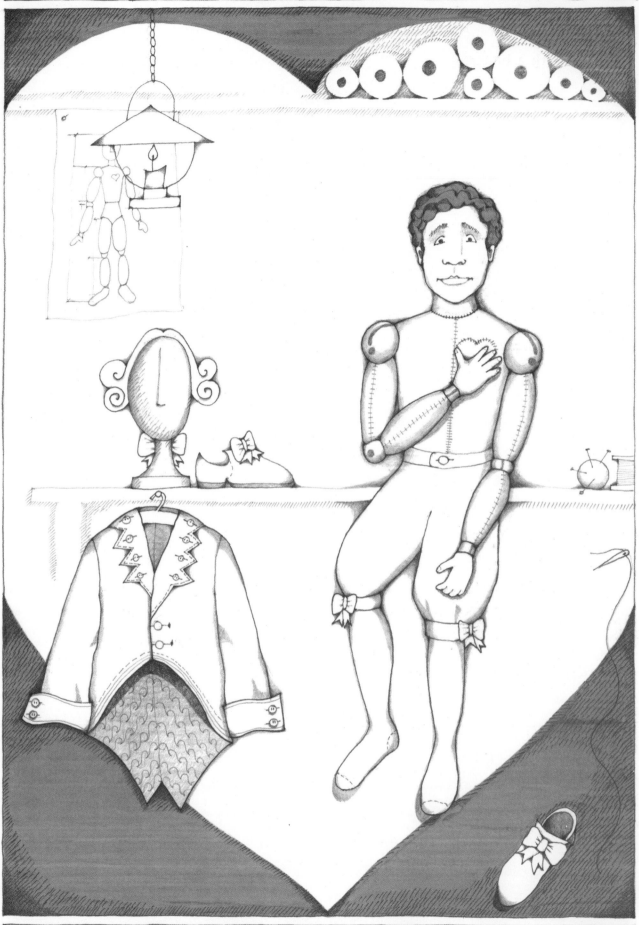

who had, at this moment rushed into the workshop with a blue velvet box. "You and your dream aren't going anywhere till I've finished my work, and we're almost late. It will take hours to button you into all your fine clothes, brush and powder your wig and shine your shoes, not to speak of teaching you your bow. And there's still your heart here to attend to. I sent off to the farthest reaches of North America for it, to a place called Texas, and thank heaven it's got here just in time. But now I must assemble it. Couldn't send you off without a heart, could we?"

Dogwood stepped forward to help her father with the tiny, intricate pieces, and then they placed the beautiful, ruby-red heart in Aethelred's chest. As the girl stitched up the supple, kid leather skin, she felt the doll's heart begin to beat beneath her fingers. Aethelred looked at Dogwood in amazement, as he had not expected his heart to beat so loudly in his chest. Dogwood, who had not expected it to beat at all, was speechless. Her eyebrows shot up like little brown seagulls over her wide set brown eyes.

"Dogwood, I don't understand. I am only a doll. How can my heart be beating so?" And Dogwood, though herself astonished, tried not to betray her surprise. For some reason, though, her face flushed and her hands shook. She dropped her tiny gold needle on the floor and brushed tears from her cheeks as she bent to break the thread with her teeth.

"Redwood, I cannot tell you why your heart is beating. Nor do I really know why my own heart beats. Perhaps it has something to do with your dream, whatever it may be. Perhaps it is something special my father has done to make you seem more human. I do not know. All I know is that I wish you did not have to go."

"But Dogwood, I must. I was made to be with the Princess Elspeth, created just for her. Still, I feel so strange, so sad. I would wish I knew why, if I hadn't already used up my only wish."

"It's getting late, Dogwood," said Tom, gently. "I must take Aethelred now and go down to the party. The King will be waiting, and I do have an uncontrollable desire to stick my toes in the River Waking. Will you come this year, my dear? It's dark now, but the air is so full of fireflies I'm sure we won't need a torch."

very year, Tom asked Dogwood to come to the party and, every year, she stayed home, somehow knowing that her presence irritated the King and Queen. The contrast between Dogwood and Elspeth was something the royal couple always found disquieting.

In their great, silver bed at night, the

King had so often said to his wife with a deep sigh, "My love, I wonder if we shouldn't have dreamed of having the kindest daughter in the kingdom instead of the prettiest."

But the Queen, equally troubled by Elspeth's tantrums and sullenness, and Dogwood's grace, had always replied, "Yes, but darling, she would probably have looked just like Tom's daughter – good, but as plain as a plate."

"Well, we're plain, aren't we?" the King would laugh, planting a kiss on the Queen's ruddy cheek, "But we do love one another." And, that said, the pair would go off to sleep, ugly, beet-red, and content, their snoring drowning out the sound of smashing toys and mirrors above them.

As it was, the royal couple rarely saw Dogwood, and never on the first of Everso at Elspeth's birthday party. Tom always went alone and left his daughter at home where she drew pictures of the party she could only hear in the distance. In all the previous years, Dogwood had enjoyed this time alone, but this year was different.

This year, on a wide piece of parchment, she drew the River Waking, and the throngs of happy children playing on its banks. She drew the tables heaped with sweets, the acrobats, the colored lights strung in the magnolias. And then she drew Aethelred, in his paisley, satin westcoat and lace stock, and his purple frock coat with its six hundred and seventy Mother of Pearl buttons.

She drew him bowing before the beautiful Elspeth. She drew him taking her hand. She drew him bending forward to kiss her cheek, and then she tore the parchment into tiny, tiny pieces, threw herself face down on her cot in the basement workshop and wept.

"Oh dear, dear," said the rocking horse, rocking back and forth in its corner. "Oh dear, dear."

At the very moment Dogwood was weeping in her father's toy shop, the King was escorting Aethelred to the Princess, with Tom following along behind, a fat sack of Dreamlanders slung over his shoulder. All

the people of Dreamland caught their breath when they saw the beautiful princeling, and no one would believe even the King when he informed them that this perfect gentleman was only a doll.

"You've outdone yourself this time, Tom," said the Queen. "I wish my sons, poor dears, looked as good. Can this handsome youth with the blush on his cheek be a toy?"

"Well, yes," said Tom, "and no," he added, remembering Aethelred's heartbeat. "Let's just say this is a doll like no other."

"I don't care what he is," squealed Elspeth, who had swooped down from her turret to claim her birthday present. She was wearing shades of purple herself this year, yards and yards of pale mauve lace and a tiara of amethysts, but she'd rushed out of her rooms so quickly that she still had one pink curler in her hair.

"He may be a doll, but he's the most beautiful, perfect thing I have ever seen! Oh, turn around, turn around!" she pealed. "Turn around for me, Aethelred!"

om and the King, stepping back from the doll, watched in pleasure as the princeling turned gracefully, bowed, and extended one lifelike hand to the Princess. Elspeth herself, wobbling in an even higher pair of purple heels, curtsied and, at that moment, the sky lit up with hundreds of purple and mauve and pink fireworks, and the great crowds on the banks of the River Waking applauded in joy. This was the one day of the year when they felt they could count on Elspeth's being happy.

"Well, lovely one, are you really pleased? Where is that little girl who said she was too old for toys, eh?" shouted the King above all the noise.

"Oh Daddy, he's a dream come true. He's the best present you've ever given me, and he's mine now, all mine," said Elspeth.

And then, her face going a bit hard, she commanded, "Aethelred! Shall I call you Prince Aethelred, since you look so much like me? Prince Aethelred, then, kiss me, kiss me! There's no harm in it, since you're just a doll. So, do kiss me, do! Now!"

Aethelred, dazzled by Elspeth's beauty, and the smoke and brilliance of the fireworks, indeed began to bend forward towards the little Princess, who was so much tinier than Dogwood. But then he stopped. He looked deep into her enormous, celery-green eyes, fringed, like his own, with licorice-black lashes, and then his new heart ceased beating.

Not only did his heart go still, but he found he could no longer speak or move. A chill had pierced him all of a sudden and he felt as cold as a bar of soap. For all his purple

satin and lace and leather, and for all the warmth of the Everso night, Prince Aethelred was shivering.

"Well, what's wrong with you?" exclaimed Elspeth in annoyance. "Didn't you hear me? Has Tom forgotten to sew on your ears?"

Tom and the King and Queen, standing close by, were the only ones to witness this little scene, and hurriedly carried the doll into the castle, where Tom bent over and put his ear to Aethelred's chest.

"I knew it was too good to be true," he moaned. "Oh Aethelred, speak to me. What's wrong, my fine lad?"

"What's wrong, indeed?" barked the King. "Tom, with all the Dreamlanders I've doled out for this toy, the least he can do is give my daughter a peck on her cheek!"

"Your Grace," sighed Tom, "I don't understand this at all, but here are your Dreamlanders until I've had time to fetch my tools and take a look at his heart. Let me move him up to Elspeth's room and you go back and enjoy the party. I've brought my screwdriver and wrench with me, and I'll see if there's something I can do. Maybe it's just the shock of a new environment. You know how plants lose their leaves when you move them, and cats go off their food. Perhaps it's only that. After all, he's never seen a princess before."

"Nonsense, Tom. I won't take even a Ha'dreamlander back. He's the most wonderful toy in the kingdom, and if all he can do is stand there, that's enough for me," roared the monarch.

"I have a very high window, though," hissed Elspeth, turning on one purple heel, "But for now I think I'll just go cool my toes and eat some of my cake. Too bad your mouth won't open, Aethelred."

o, Elspeth's brothers carried the princeling the ten stories up to their little sister's rooms and stood him next to the turret window where he could look out over the dark fields, the party lights, the emerald

river and, in the distance, see the toy maker's cottage.

While Tom tinkered with his chest, Aethelred gazed out. There was a light in the toyshop's basement window – Dogwood's candle – and when the doll saw this light the color crept back into his cheeks and he found he could speak.

"Tom, I don't know what's got into me or, rather, what's gone out of me," he began, but Tom interrupted.

"Well, my boy, I don't either, but I can tell you that displeasing Princess Elspeth is a dangerous business. Isn't she beautiful? Don't you like her?" Tom's face had drained of color and he was perspiring from the long climb and from worry.

Aethelred answered honestly. "Yes, it is true she is beautiful – the most beautiful creature I shall ever see. But no, Tom, I don't like her at all, and I will never, ever kiss her."

The toy maker sighed, sadly thinking of all the work he and Dogwood had put into making Aethelred. The Dreamlanders would be in the bank in the morning, but he hated to imagine the princeling in pieces at the foot of Elspeth's turret. He shuddered and turned to go, but then came back across the room to look at his creation one last time.

"About your dream, Aethelred," he began. "I assume you have one?"

"Yes," answered the doll, absently. "I

do. My dream is to love and serve the most perfect creature in all of Dreams-upon-Waking, to love and cherish her alone. Is that not Elspeth? The way you described her, I was so certain it was Elspeth. Was I wrong? Were you wrong?"

om, stung to the quick, suddenly found himself thinking of a plate-plain, gangly girl, her hair tied back with a strand of blue yarn. In a daze, he stumbled down the flights and flights of stone steps, Dreamlanders spilling behind him, and rushed home.

When he arrived, Dogwood was asleep, the candle in her window burned down to a nub and guttering in its holder. "Oh Dogwood," he whispered hoarsely, catching her up in his arms, "What have I done? He was like the son I never had, and I fear I've sent him to his death. But what am I saying? He's a doll, isn't he? Oh Dogwood, tell me he's only a doll!"

But Dogwood, opening her eyes on her father's distraught face, could not comfort him. She had heard Aethelred's heart beating as her own heart beat. Instead, she went to the window, blew out her candle and looked up sternly at the turret where Elspeth lived. She knew what she must do.

From that night onwards, after the lamp lighter had made his way through the town,

filling all the lanterns on the street corners with fireflies, Dogwood would creep silently out of the workshop, along with the toy soldier, the ballerina and the rocking horse. She'd attached four roller skates to the rocking horse's runners, and the toy soldier helped her pull the horse along the road up to the castle.

Night after night, the four would keep watch in the dark beneath Elspeth's window. There was a shallow hole in the ground on the lawn there, which they stood well away from, and here they would wait, all through the month of Everso, for what they knew was coming.

Elspeth, away up in her tower, paced back and forth every evening, practicing twirls with her little silver baton, every now and then giving her full length mirror a smart little rap which added yet another crack to its already cracked surface. Elspeth's mirror dreamed of reflecting the beauty of the dawn sky, and so had never been of any use to Elspeth, who merely wanted a mirror to tell her if her tiara was on straight or her petticoat showing.

But the mirror didn't regret its choice of a dream, for it was spared reflecting the sight of the pitiful Aethelred, standing so mournfully by the window. There he stood, as still as a stick, day after day, not even flinching when Elspeth tossed a slipper at him or shouted in his ear.

"One little kiss, you big, tall, purple-covered coat hanger!" she would shriek. "Is that too much for a princess to ask? Oh nobody cares what I want," she'd pout, collapsing in an overstuffed chair. "Daddy's got his money back, my birthday's over, I won't get any more presents till Christmas, and just look at you. You're about as useful as my mirror, and a great deal bulkier. Just another piece of useless furniture to dust. I've a good mind to throw you out the window! Yes, that's just what I shall do!"

It wasn't at all easy to get Aethelred out the narrow window, but Elspeth had built up some strong little arms twirling her baton and whacking her mirror all those years, not to speak of hurling heavy objects out of the tower, so on the last day of Everso, just when the sky was becoming overcast with the first rain clouds of the season, and a stiff breeze had come up, the Princess managed to lift the doll up in her arms and tilt him over the window sill.

Aethelred, looking down in the deepening darkness, thought he saw Dogwood standing beneath him and a smile flickered on his lips just before he plummeted headfirst into the night.

Elspeth slammed the window behind him and turned to her mirror. "Well, what are you

gawking at?" she yelled, momentarily waking her parents nine stories beneath her. "He was only a doll!"

But the King, who discovered Aethelred's absence in her rooms the next morning, and knew what had transpired the night before, had had enough of his daughter's tantrums. "I don't care if he was just straw and leather, my girl!" he roared. "Enough is enough! That boy – er, that toy – was the handsomest thing I have ever seen, and you ought to be ashamed of yourself, chucking him out the window like that. From now on, you're to stay in your rooms. No more presents! No more parties! No more anything until you change your ways. And hand me that baton! I'm taking this poor mirror away, too. Four hundred Dreamlanders for this looking glass and it looks as if someone's been practicing the drums on it!"

The King in his distress then hurried down to collect the unfortunate Aethelred's remains but, as with the earlier toys, he found nothing on the castle lawn except some curious wheel marks and a few shreds of purple satin.

Back at the toy shop, Dogwood was her same sweet self by day, helping her father and doing her chores, though Tom noticed she always seemed tired, and dark circles ringed her eyes. Still, she seemed happier than she had been during the month of Everso, and she never seemed to mind staying home in the evening when Tom would go out to visit with his friends.

After dark, when she went down to the basement to sleep, Dogwood would light a candle and then bring Prince Aethelred out from behind the screen, assisted by her faithful trio of friends. When they had brought him back from the castle, Aethelred had been a horrible sight, every porcelain limb broken, every beautiful garment torn. He had been soaked with rain and unrecognizable, except for a fixed smile on his silent lips.

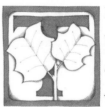he very next day, Dogwood had begun the painstaking work of repairing the damage. She worked alone now, without her father's expert guidance, but in her thirteen years in the shop, she had learned every facet of the trade. The job would take twice as long, she knew, years perhaps, but she would make Redwood whole again.

"You'll see, my Prince," she would tell him, for she always spoke to him while she stitched and glued and stuffed, as though he could still hear her. "You'll be better than before – some day."

In fact, her labor took years to complete. Tom had grown rich and fat and hardly ever entered the work room, and Dogwood

Perhaps I just didn't watch carefully enough all those years ago when he made you."

It took the girl another hour to stitch up the prince's chest and arrange his clothing. By the time she had finished, Dogwood was so tired she sat down and fell asleep in a chair, her head bent over the work table where she had seated the prince.

As the sun rose and the bright light of an Everso dawn crept across the floor and fell upon the table, Aethelred opened his eyes and looked down on Dogwood's tousled hair and wondered if he were dreaming.

"Dogwood, is it you?" he whispered, his unused voice breaking and the unused words coming back to him as though from a great distance. "Dogwood, wake up, wake up! I have something to tell you!"

Dogwood, hearing the familiar, beloved voice, raised her head and looked up at Aethelred; then rose to her feet and reached out her hands to him.

"Dogwood, I know now why I could not bring myself to kiss Princess Elspeth, and why I went so cold inside when she spoke to me. My dream, dearest Dogwood, which I decided upon the night before I left you, was to love and cherish and serve the most perfect creature in Dreamland, and that creature, Dogwood, is you, and will always be you. I just didn't know it till now."

Aethelred went down on one stiff knee

herself had changed from a gangling girl into a young woman. Still plain, she was more graceful than before. She was blooming and in her sixteenth year the night she decided to attempt the repair of the doll's ruby heart.

It took hours and hours to assemble all the tiny pieces of gemstone, and hours to decipher the directions for assembly, which were printed in Javanese on the original box. For all Dogwood's efforts, the heart, once repaired, remained as still as the night. "Oh Redwood, it's no use. Only my father can make your heart beat again, and I can't even tell him you're here. Oh how I wish I had his skill. I wish I knew how to repair hearts.

then, and took Dogwood's hands in his own, then raised them to his lips. And, at that moment, his ruby heart filled to bursting and began, once again, to beat. Tears welled up in his eyes, and the kid leather of his hands and the porcelain of his face turned to warm, living flesh.

ogwood's father, who had come down the steps when he heard an almost forgotten voice in the basement, watched the doll's transformation occur before his very eyes, but still could not believe what he had witnessed.

"Dogwood, what have you done, my girl? Is this not Aethelred, the toy we fashioned for Princess Elspeth? But how does a doll made of stuffing and leather live and breathe?"

". . . and love," murmured Dogwood. "He does because I dreamed that this doll might, one day, become human, and never again be commanded by a spoiled little girl, or be hurled from a ten story window. He lives because Redwood is a dream come true, my heart's desire."

Tom, knowing Aethelred's dream, and now his daughter's as well, looked at them both in wonder. "Never have I seen a doll more noble, a girl more giving," he babbled happily.

"I think," said Aethelred, "while I'm down here on my knee, I shall ask your daughter to marry me, Tom."

"And I think," laughed Dogwood, "I shall not let him up till he *has* asked, if you have no objection, Daddy."

"Well, I have no objection at all," said Tom, but I think we might put the wedding off at least till tomorrow, for we're going to be late for the party and, in Dreamland, that just won't do."

"Ah yes," said Dogwood thoughtfully. "It's the first of Everso, and Elspeth's seventeenth birthday, though she's been locked up in her turret for almost three years now without seeing a soul. Still, the King and Queen have carried on the annual celebration in the hope that their daughter's hard little heart will soften. But, as I understand it, she's still the same as ever, though she's had no toys to toss out her window since my dear Redwood here."

"A good thing!" piped up the rocking horse, who'd forgotten that Tom was in the room.

"Well, what have we here?" said Tom, in further amazement. "Dogwood, if you've done what I think you've done, you've performed miracles down here alone in the dark. But these three toys were bought and paid for by Their Royal Majesties and should, by all rights, be returned to the King."

"Oh dear, dear," cried the rocking horse.

"I'll go, of course, but you must promise me, Dogwood, that you'll give us all parachutes this time."

t was the most beautiful day of the year, in fact the most beautiful day the people of Dreamland could remember, and it was to be the sweetest, most remarkable day in the kingdom's history.

Other countries would remember their terrible battles, their hard-won victories and their heroes' great deeds with holidays. The people of Dreamland would remember the day a doll became a prince, a prince married a toy maker's daughter, a princess became a queen and a king arrived on a quest.

In Dreams-upon-Waking, the first of Everso would be celebrated ever after as Dogwood Day. But, as my mother said at this point, "I'm getting ahead of my story. First, I must tell you about the party."

For Elspeth's seventeenth birthday, the people of Dreamland had outdone themselves. The King and Queen had been so sad for all the years their youngest daughter had been locked up in her tower that they'd actually become thin and pink when before they had always been fat and red. Their subjects had baked and baked for months all the tempting sweets they could think of in the hope of fattening up the royal family again.

Elspeth's brothers and sisters, all married now, with some twenty-eight grandchildren – most homely as roots – to show for their happy unions, had all arrived from kingdoms near and far, but they too were a little glum. Still, the people were looking forward to the fireworks, which were rumored to have cost the King some two thousand Dreamlanders.

When Tom, Dogwood, Aethelred and the three mended toys arrived at the castle, everyone was out on the lawn playing croquet and badminton and touch football, but when they saw the toy maker's perfect princeling, so obviously human now, they dropped their mallets and rackets and even the football in

disbelief. The King and Queen were sent for and when they arrived they immediately came up to Tom and the little band and stood with pink mouths open as Dogwood related the story of the prince's great fall, her own years of work, and the coming true of her fondest dream. The King gave the young couple his blessing then and the Queen found it in her heart to kiss Dogwood and tell her she only wished Elspeth had dreamed so fine a dream. "I don't know what's to become of her," she said, looking up at the high, bright window.

The rocking horse, the toy soldier and the ballerina were then brought forward, quaking in fear, but the King said that under no circumstances would they ever be given back to Elspeth. "I think," said the King, "that my twenty-eight, or is it twenty-nine, grandchildren will be much more appreciative of you in the years to come, and so you shall stay in your own quarters until they are old enough to enjoy you when they come to visit."

"Oh dear, thank you," said the rocking horse, rocking contentedly.

"I am sworn to protect the crown, Your Grace," said the toy soldier, and the ballerina executed a neat pirouette on one toe which had all the little girls, royal and common alike, trying to imitate her.

It was at just this moment that there came a terrible shriek from the turret. "Let me out

of here! Let me out, do you hear! If someone doesn't come up here this instant and unlock this door, I'm going to jump!"

"Oh dear," said the rocking horse, "and she doesn't even have a parachute!"

The great crowd went as silent as the sky just after lightning strikes, and then Elspeth's mother began to cry noisily. "Oh please don't, Elspeth darling! I'm coming up at once, dear!" This said, she rushed off into the castle, blowing her nose in a fuschia handkerchief.

But before the throng of subjects dressed in their best party clothes had had time to turn to one another and say a word, a trumpet sounded from down river where the magnolia forest began, and then a company of knights on horseback appeared at a canter, followed by a very royal personage indeed, mounted on a rather winded grey stallion.

Tom, who'd spent a lifetime studying the costumes and heraldry of various royal households, found his voice then and said quietly to his sovereign, "Sire, it's the young king of Lux-upon-Terra. Yes, I do believe it's the young Clovis himself, for though he's the spitting image of his rotund father, also a rather homely fellow with quite a bald pate, he can't be a day over twenty."

Elspeth was still shrieking from her turret and now had one lovely leg out the window, but the Queen could be heard puffing up

the stairs to the tower rooms. Just to be safe, the rocking horse was rocking away from the gentle depression in the lawn just underneath the Princess's window, but it was here that Clovis dismounted, leaping gracefully – for one his size – off his horse, which sighed loudly in relief.

ing Clovis then came up to the King of Dreamland to pay his respects, hand extended, his face all smiles. Paying respects was a bit difficult just at this moment, as Elspeth was screeching at the top of her lungs and it was impossible to ignore her and talk casually about such things as the weather, the rising of the rivers Waking and Terra, and other matters.

Finally, King Clovis was forced to abandon the expected pleasantries and remarked, cocking his head back, "I say, who is that gorgeous young woman up there with her legs out the window, and why is she making such a fuss? Can that be the Princess Elspeth, whose beauty is spoken of even in distant Lux-upon-Terra?"

Because King Clovis was not a handsome man, but so obviously a candid and approachable one, Dogwood stepped forward and curtsied.

"Oh bother curtsying!" he bellowed. "It always makes me think someone's suddenly stepped into a hole and then bobbed up again like a duck! You're Dogwood, aren't you? Your people all call you Dogwood the Good. Did you know that?"

"No," replied Dogwood, though she was very surprised, and her eyebrows flew up. "But I fear Princess Elspeth the Fair, if also the Impossible, may shortly become Elspeth the Flat if something isn't done, Your Majesty!"

"You see, my fine fellow," said the King of Dreamland unhappily, "my daughter's chosen an impossible dream. Everyone must do her bidding for her to be happy, and I'm afraid, considering other people have dreams of their own, Elspeth's course in life hasn't been easy, for her or anyone else."

"It was, in fact, my downfall," said the rocking horse.

"Only one dream allowed here, eh?" asked King Clovis, grinning through the mass of red beard he'd grown to make up for his shiny pink head.

"Why yes," said Aethelred. "One dream is all we're granted in life."

King Clovis pondered this a moment and then reared back on his heels and roared. "Elspeth! Come down here!"

He needn't have yelled for at this precise instant Elspeth and the Queen behind her were just spilling out the castle door in a cloud of red, pink and gold tulle. Elspeth was as pale as a candle but was dressed for her

birthday party in golden net, yards and yards of it. She was wearing her ceremonial crown and was quite breathtakingly beautiful in her anger and freedom. She looked like a tigress let out of a cage.

"And who might you be, you bald-headed bear, to order a princess about?" she snapped, rising to her not great height and squinting up at King Clovis.

lovis threw back his big red-bearded head again at this and laughed out loud, though the King and Queen of Dreamland were mortified and Dogwood and Aethelred exchanged sad glances, knowing Elspeth's ways all too well.

"I, my loudmouthed little doll, am King Clovis, known as Clovis the Great for reasons obvious to my poor tailor and my longsuffering horse here. And in Lux-upon-Terra, my kingdom and my father's kingdom before me, far to the north, I have been pining away for the wife I intend to make of you one fine day!"

This was a mouthful, but Clovis obviously had no problem delivering long-winded speeches.

"What!" squeaked Elspeth. "Me? The beautiful, the exquisite Elspeth marry a great florid hulk like you!"

"Now, now, dear," said the Queen, stifling a grin, "Your father was once a great florid hulk, and I married him." The King of Dreamland was grinning himself, his hand reaching out even then for a cinnamon bun on a nearby table.

"My plan precisely," boomed Clovis.

"And just how do you propose to change my mind about accepting your offer? Tell me that, sir! Because I can tell you I have no intention of becoming Queen Elspeth of Lux-upon-Whatsit." Geography had never been Elspeth's strongest subject.

"Well," said the young monarch thoughtfully, "Lux-upon-Terra's quite a different place than your Dreamland here."

"How so?" asked Dogwood quietly.

"In Lux, my good Dogwood, we are all granted two dreams at birth. We may make two wishes and both will be fulfilled; the first one for ourselves, and the second for someone else."

"How wonderful," said Aethelred, hugging Dogwood to him. "How lovely!"

"Well, yes," said Clovis, eyeing Elspeth, "But you can still dream perfectly rotten dreams just like Elspeth's here and end up in a muddle. Still, it sometimes works out delightfully."

"And what are your dreams, Your Grace," asked Dogwood, earnestly, "If you don't mind telling us, that is?"

"Fine lass you've got there, Aethelred.

Fine, bright lass! Well, my first dream, Dogwood, was to become a wise, wise man. From childhood, when I sat at my bald and homely but wise father's knee, all I desired was to become wiser and wiser and wiser. And I suppose, given the amount of time I spend laughing and chuckling and smiling per day, I must indeed be becoming wise."

"Oh yes, he is very wise," said the knights accompanying King Clovis. "We and everyone else in Lux can attest to that. The whole kingdom has benefited from his wisdom and mirth."

"I do hope so," said Clovis calmly, turning to look at Elspeth, who was now calm herself, and staring back up at him. "It has been my only dream . . . till now. Till now, Elspeth my dear, because I have now, at last, met the person for whom I shall wish my second wish."

"Oh no you don't," breathed Elspeth, but you could tell her heart wasn't in it. Clovis then took both her translucent hands in his big bear-like paws, as gently as a mother cat lifts a kitten in her teeth. "Oh no!"

"Oh yes," laughed Clovis tenderly.

"For I shall close my eyes now and wish that you, as my wife, become far wiser even than I, as wise as you are beautiful. Going down on one knee on your father's lawn here, I will wish that you give up your tiny, terrible dream, the dream that has kept you a prisoner far more cruelly than any turret room. That you will ride out into the sunlight tomorrow morning on a beautiful grey stallion which will so appreciate carrying a light, lovely burden such as yourself. Oh Elspeth, be mine!"

"Oh my, oh no, oh yes!" sighed Elspeth, fainting.

"Oh wonderful!" said Clovis, catching her.

"Oh dear, oh dear!" piped up the rocking horse happily.

"And is that where the story ends, Mother?" I asked, for it was getting late, and I had to be at school early the next day.

"No, Sweet Pea. That's where the story begins. For that very night there was the great double wedding of King Clovis and Princess Elspeth, and Dogwood the Good and Prince Aethelred. And then King Clovis and Elspeth rode away to the north the next day to rule Lux-upon-Terra, and Dogwood and Aethelred moved into the castle where Dogwood the Good became heir to the throne of Dreamland, by popular demand and royal decree, and every one of them lived long and happily, and the King and Queen became fat and jolly again and the first of Everso was celebrated year after year after year, and Tom made toys for all of Dogwood's homely little children to play with."

"And did Dogwood ever become beautiful?" I would ask, finally, pulling the blue yarn from my hair as I settled down to sleep for the night.

"Well, you know, it's funny you should ask that. The King gave Dogwood Elspeth's old mirror when she and Aethelred moved into the rooms at the top of the turret, and it was then that Dogwood first saw her own face."

"And do you know what she said, Sweet Pea, when she looked into the mirror? She said, 'Oh, darling Redwood, why didn't anyone ever tell me that I look just as lovely as the dawn sky?'"

T H E   E N D

THE PAPER DOLLS

Please photocopy Dogwood and Elspeth onto heavy
card stock at 150 percent of their original size. Then
photocopy their wardrobes onto regular printer paper,
also at 150 percent. Color brightly, cut out and play!

DOGWOOD

ELSPETH

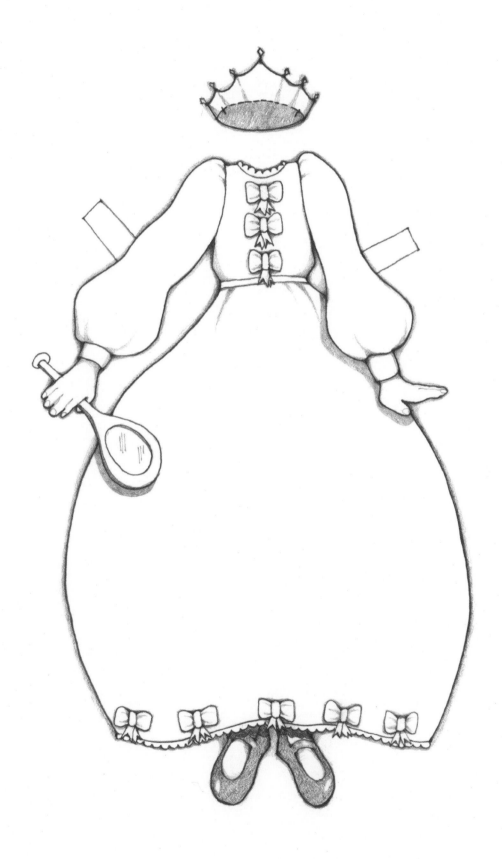

A B O U T   T H I S   B O O K

"This is the second of my children's stories to be dreamed, and written down upon waking, in Greece. *The First of Everso* came to be one spring night on the island of Santorini, where I had gone, accompanied by my mother, Beth, to write a guide book to the Cyclades. We slept, overlooking the still active volcano and, in the night, I was visited by Dogwood and Elspeth, Aethelred and Clovis, and a rollerskating rocking horse. Like many of my generation, I suspect that much of who and what we are we choose to be, choose to become. So we must, willy nilly, examine our choices with care: we will inhabit them for some time; and they had better 'become' us . . . ."

Elizabeth Boleman-Herring

ABOUT THE AUTHOR

Elizabeth Boleman-Herring was born in North Carolina, but spent the first nine years of her life in Pasadena, California. At 10, she moved with her parents to Greece where her father was posted as a Fulbright scholar at Pierce College. Educated at the American Community Schools of Athens, the Francis W. Parker School of Chicago, the University of Georgia, the University of South Carolina, and at American University, Boleman-Herring returned to Greece as an adult to pursue a career in letters. She served as Deputy Editor of *The Athenian: Greece's English Language Monthly* and became founder and Publishing Editor of *The Southeastern Review: A Quarterly Journal of the Humanities in the Southeastern Mediterranean*. Her first children's book, *The Other Side of the Road*, was published, in a first US edition, by The Literate Chigger Press. Boleman-Herring's poetry has appeared in numerous publications, as have her columns, features, reviews, jazz lyrics, photographs and travel articles. A collection of her poetry, *The Crowded Bed: Light and Formal Verse*, was published by Lycabettus Press, and her travel guides to Greece, its islands and Athens for Insight Guides have been issued in many editions. With photographer Clay Perry, she wrote *Vanishing Greece* and, in 2004, at www.greecetraveler.com, she launched the online travel guide and website, *Elizabeth Boleman-Herring's Greece: The Thinking Traveler's Guide to Hellas*. Boleman-Herring divides her time between homes in New Jersey and the Greek islands, traveling to and fro with her husband, jazz trumpeter Dean Pratt.

ABOUT THE ILLUSTRATOR

Sandra Tice-Wright is just one of a family full of musicians, writers and artists, and so she is loath to tout her talents. For her, art is simply a way of life. After three years of studying architecture with an emphasis in visual arts, she took a hiatus actually to work within the architectural community: But it proved to be too many straight lines! Luckily, she wasn't fired for all her arabesques in the margins. Tice-Wright returned to school, specializing in landscape design, continuing to be drawn to courses in visual arts, architecture, and art history. Since graduating, she has been a freelance landscape designer, a storyteller, a horticultural instructor, a private art tutor, a language arts and pre-school teacher and, currently, substitute-teaches Grades K through 5 (in anything but PT and computing). Tice-Wright shares her home in Clemson, South Carolina with her two children, her three fat cats, and one hyper dog. Other than teaching (her love), she spends her time gardening, writing, playing her violin (occasionally), and her bongos (frequently). Her now-almost-grown children, Ben and Hannah, were the models for Aethelred and Dogwood.

ABOUT THE DESIGNER

Gareth Walters was born in Mexborough, South Yorkshire, UK and has worked in the graphic design industry for 25 years. Following periods in London, Athens (where he first met the author), Munich and Hong Kong, he now lives and works as a Creative Director in Menlo Park, California.